Crown of Weeds

Also by Amy Gerstler

The True Bride
Primitive Man
Past Lives (with Alexis Smith)
Bitter Angel
Nerve Storm

Amy Gerstler

Crown of Weeds

Penguin Poets

PENGUIN BOOKS

Published by the Penguin Group

Penguin Books USA Inc., 375 Hudson Street, New York, New York 10014, U.S.A.

Penguin Books Ltd, 27 Wrights Lane, London W8 5TZ, England

Penguin Books Australia Ltd, Ringwood, Victoria, Australia

Penguin Books Canada Ltd, 10 Alcorn Avenue, Toronto, Ontario, Canada M4V 3B2

Penguin Books (N.Z.) Ltd, 182–190 Wairau Road, Auckland 10, New Zealand

Penguin Books Ltd, Registered Offices: Harmondsworth, Middlesex, England

First published in Penguin Books 1997

1   3   5   7   9   10   8   6   4   2

Page ix constitutes an extension of this copyright page.

LIBRARY OF CONGRESS CATALOGING IN PUBLICATION DATA

Gerstler, Amy.

Crown of weeds/Amy Gerstler.

p.   cm.—(Penguin poets)

ISBN 0 14 058.778 0

I. Title.

PS3557.E735C76   1997

811'.54—dc20   96–31902

Printed in the United States of America

Set in Centaur MT

Designed by Junie Lee

for Marcus Gerstler

Acknowledgments

Thanks to the following people for their support:
Dennis Cooper, Michelle Huneven, Alexis Smith, Megan
Williams, Benjamin Weissman, Tina Gerstler, Sid and
Mimi Gerstler, David Trinidad, Ira Silverberg, Michael
Ryan, Tom Knechtel, Tom Clark.

Some of the poems in this collection were previously
published in the following magazines, some in slightly
different form:
*Alaska Quarterly Review, American Letters and Commentary,
American Poetry Review, The American Voice, Antioch Review,
Arshile, ArtCommotion, Chelsea, Colorado Review, Columbia,
Columbia Poetry Review, Gulf Coast, Lingo, Los Angeles Times
Book Review, Long Shot, New American Writing, Ruby, The San
Diego Reader, San Francisco State University Review,* and *The World.*

Contents

Crown of Weeds

Recipe for Resurrection

Bathe the body in quinine.
Then let his wrists
be braceleted with the stings
of tiny iridescent insects.
A group of ten restless boys
should encircle the sleeper
whose marrow is to be rekindled.
The boys must sneeze violently
without covering their mouths
till the body is wet.
A poultice of figs and licorice
smeared over the lips
has often proved useful.
Rub foot soles with prickly poppy
and buttermilk. Place a live
green tree frog over each nipple
and stroke the frogs tenderly
until they are calm. Cover the empty
genitals with white duck feathers.
Allow relatives to huff and puff
and blow the feathers away.
Under no circumstances should
anyone sweep them up or collect them.
They must float where they will.

Don't let the sleeper stand up
too quickly. Giddy on arising,
he may declare there are swarms
of fireflies swooping through
the room. He'll be hoarse,

prey for days to seaside
complaints, prone to whine
that everything smells of vinegar
(or another pickling solution),
and that, sore all over, nothing
he lies down on is soft enough
anymore. He may try to bite you.
He might talk nonsense, and sob:
Where is the silver forest,
the lapping glassy canal
unruffled by its boats,
the flock of noisy parrots
I was promised?
Resist the temptation
to fall to your knees
and beg his forgiveness. Instead,
armed with pinches and kisses,
fistfuls of pumpkin seeds
and biscuit crumbs, let him
be breathed on by the subtle
dusty gusts from a lily's
golden-tonsilled throat.
Graciously welcome the truant
soul home as you stutter your love—
that thin tuneless exhaust
we exhale every day.

To a Newborn

When we first met
a week ago, you were
two days old,
twenty inches long,
swaddled like a sultan,
weighing in at seven
pounds. You looked
like a furious, skinned
kitten. You looked cooked.
Roasted, to be precise.
I assume you'll cool.
I liked you enormously, due
to my affinity for anyone
pissed off, particularly
infants. The tuft of black
hair on your head seemed
magnetized. Fine as coal
dust, it stands straight
up, like a smoky flame,
a rooster's comb, a hand
raised for permission to speak.
I'd like a piece of your mind
tout de suite, so hurry
and learn English. You have
the aura of someone who's
just run a great distance.
When I see your soft,
severe, inebriated-
looking face, I become
unreasonably happy,

tearful (as you often are),
and feel completely at sea.
You seem to like to keep
only one eye open at a time,
as you twist in your mother's
arms and punch the air,
which makes you look cocky.
I own earrings bigger
than your fists. We adults
take turns smelling your
powder-scented head.

Protector of all beings,
twirling your awful lasso
of snakes, look down
on this new creature
the color of blood,
with his constantly empty stomach
and his expression as wonderfully
sour as onions sautéed in aged
yak butter. Voracious deity,
keep one of your thousand eyes
on this male baby as he picks
his way among mournful trees
and flowering plants that form
the forest of his circumstances
and family. Help him find
his true root. Do this at the most
humble request of one so terrified
(o, *trailblazer, lord of conflicting*

emotions, teacher of naked ascetics,
traveler ever arriving),
that the list of her fears would
weary to death anyone reading this
sentence, were she to mention them
all.

Circus Girl

When the gilded train stopped to fuel in a lily field,
a pretty girl, who did arabesques on the elephant's
head, and also worked as the cook's assistant,
disembarked alone. *Good-bye nightmarish high-wire
lessons. So long white tigers. Adieu jugglers
juggling rubber hatchets and glasses of buttermilk.*
Her small backpack contained an onion sandwich,
collapsible stilts, worn-out point slippers, a canteen
filled with pink lemonade, and a handful of Jumbo's
stiff whiskers, long as broom straws, tied up
in a ribbon. She passed miles of yellowing lettuce
planted in neat rows and regiments of corn stalks,
whom she saluted. *That dull-colored building
must be the schoolhouse.* She sat for a while
on the rim of a gravel quarry filled with water,
inhaling the thought-provoking smell of manure.
Spring and summer nights, it was her duty to sing
the pachyderms to sleep, then tickle them awake
at dawn with a wisp of alfalfa. "I am the one
who got away," she hummed gravely, and slapped
at a deerfly who left a welt on her arm.
Nimbly, she climbed a tree and hung upside down
from a leafy limb. *No more giant and dwarf
duets about the perils of bubble gum. Never
again a midnight chat with the snake lady.*
"Deserter!" trumpets a voice in her head.
A thousand doubts make her skin prickle. She drops
lightly to the ground. Forlorness wells up
in her lungs, makes her gasp like an asthmatic
as she remembers the puckered face of Tattoo Boy,

the contortionist, who tried to kiss her under
the bandstand that rainy day. Is there any remedy
for his terrible clumsiness? Elephants are more
delicate. Could she teach him to close his eyes
at the right moment, instead of staring himself
cross-eyed? Will the monkeys miss her? Running
at top speed, she reverses her journey, ablaze
with fear. A whistle and a loud industrial hiss.
Her train's just leaving. The sword swallower
extends one of his long arms, and after a couple
of tries, he yanks her aboard as the locomotive gains
speed, as one of the clowns wets his pants laughing.

Travel Diary

Every other avenue exhausted,
I drifted from the interstate
onto a tangle of back roads
and came to rest at the edge
of a poppy field. Its bliss-tinged
unscented orange glow was seamed
in green, its fiery perimeter
bright enough to fry the linings
of my eyes. The ocean nearby
smelled like black tea steeping.
My thoughts had the texture
of potato puree. I felt kindled,
broke, inconsolable. Pillars
of smoke rose in the distance.
Later, while being fingerprinted
at the police station, I didn't
miss for a minute the bland
apple-scented foliage of home.

Recipe for Trouble

In an empty bathroom
with a good echo, wipe
and slice some young
cucumbers while screaming
at the top of your lungs:
"I've boned more chickens
than you've ever even seen!"
Wash your hands in a nicely
flavored meat stock
while listening to radio
accounts of investigators
searching a muddy bean field
for clues to the cause
of a major plane wreck.
Bruise some shallots.
Bring the shallots
and cucumbers into the kitchen
and put them down the garbage
disposal. Leave it running
for mood music. Bone
yet another frying hen
and throw her out the window
into your creepy neighbor's
garden, where she'll regain
feathers, innards, and skeleton,
cackle back to life, and start
pecking bugs off the shrubs.
Then whip up a batch of
really eggy French toast.
Lay sections from a letter

that was never responded
to on top of the hot toast
slices and pour melted butter
over each. Take the handkerchief
of a pastor who's recently
delivered a beautiful
tear-jerking eulogy
and boil till gelatinous.
Skim off the grease.
Serve with looter's spittle,
croutons, the eyelashes of a man
who hallucinates nonstop,
slices of peeled lemon,
and a glass of port wine.

Asylum

After decades of torment
we fled. The provisional
maps had been torn up.
We escaped in a boat
built secretly
in a grove of trees.
Coming ashore, we immediately
strayed too far afield,
as newcomers and dunderheads
will do, following traces
of every rutted ghost
of a road,
overgrown with twisted,
splintering, contradictory
logic, brambles and thistles.

The men's mustaches froze.
We lived as best we could
for some months, joints
stiff with homesickness.
Even turmoil eventually
settles into relatively
fixed patterns. A vague whiteness
looming this minute to our right
could be a flock of untended
goats, a salt flat, an ash heap,
a lake of sour cream, descended
clouds, a pond frothy with the scum
of past actions—another infestation
straight from the annals of unthinkable

behavior. The landscape is changing.
Have we reached that mythical
leached-out haven where criminals
and debtors are exempt from arrest,
a zone where doctors are safe
from the patients they've maimed?
We never thought we'd chase
birds for food, use dictionaries
as kindling. Hooliganism is pooling
just ahead, and diplomatic silence
forms a tidal wave behind us.
I hope that our enemies
or our friends will come
to their senses.

Ash Wednesday

Tonight's furious celibate weather—
a long awaited downpour—
frees slugs and earthworms,
lubricates their pathways
and destinations. Streams
sizzle and swell. Someone
is thinking of you without
being aware of it.
He starts up from bed
as if awakened by sirens
or an explosion—but these
are only echoes of sounds
the walls sucked up long ago,
now loosened by lightning.
The wind's blowing the wrong
direction. Rain has made
the air smell like soggy
cardboard and fermented plums.
He listens to the rain drum
and imagines his house washed
from its foundation,
borne like a clumsy boat
through surging floodwaters.
He pictures himself straddling
its pitched roof, rushed north
by the storm, floating for days
wrapped in blankets, holding
a kerosene lamp. Neighbors bob by
and wave. The pleasures of love
are lost on this man. A few

suits in the back of his closet
are so covered with moths
the furry white insects
look like a fabric design.
He finds love full of frustration
and change, a bumpy ride,
not the ideal accord he'd been
led to expect. Dozing again,
he dreams all his teeth are loose.
You appear in this dream,
a troublesome image,
walking his dog while having
a good cry, trying to wipe
your nose on the leash. Then
the scene shifts to his family farm
where they make Roquefort cheese—
it's iris-picking time.
Fruit you'd given him when
the two of you were still
speaking sits in a blue bowl
on the nightstand as he snores:
four huge oranges, a red pear,
purple, marble-sized grapes.
He dreams his watch is embedded
in his wrist. Ice forms
on the lettuce in your dark
garden. There's a certain wild
sadness inherent in this season.
The never-said gathers momentum,
like coming thunder. You cannot

have his precious attention.
No fever will break, no peace
be declared. The time is ripe
to walk out, soul intact,
onto the balcony in your nightgown,
get wet and soak up the thrilling
silence, but you're not ready yet.

Bedlam

I was brought here to recover
my presence of mind—
a pear-scented essence
which slipped through my fingers
like disobedient lotion,
pressed from glow-in-the-dark azaleas
nurtured in church basements.
Looks like somebody goofed, though.
The usual amenities
have proved less than theraputic,
though we're provided with brocade
fainting couches now,
prodded to talk about
how it feels to be run over
repeatedly by late model cars.
Each of our sneezes
is captured on film
and screened for our families
on visitors' day.
Squirrels scamper
all over the grounds.
They come so close to my window
I can see their tiny sex organs
and monitor their hyper gnawings.
They tunnel through an apple
in under thirty seconds.
Nor are the thin unkissable lips
of the Nazi youth turned theologian
incarcerated next door a harmless sight,

as he mouthes songs about turtles
and shrimp slugging it out
in the warm waters
of the Gulf of Mexico.
No one will lift a finger to help me.
Yesterday, a doctor asked what I was
willing to give up to get well.
Daddy's moonshine?
The gun on the nightstand?
My rumpled piety? I'm not picky,
but what *was* last night's
mysterious entrée, anyway,
blanketed with that insane
dill-flecked homemade mayonnaise?
My next door neighbor is dead set
on converting me this mild morning,
though I've already told him
I've had one toe dipped
into his personal version
of the lapping afterlife for years,
and I find it less than temperate.
I listen to his melodramatic harangues
all through breakfast, trying to keep
the fireball of my attention
from shooting out of my head,
busting through the picture window,
and incinerating the nearby pines.
We all lose ourselves sometimes.
But to render true service to another,

one must serve him without relinquishing
oneself. Easier said than done.
This spreading darkness is not entirely
mine. The dinged-up cafeteria ceiling
leads me to believe that though it's likely
I contracted my malady from the would-be
preacher, if I remain committed and vigilant,
my thoughts will soon reconvene
with more gravity than ever,
laced with caramelized terror,
delicately flavored with geranium.

April

The slate stepping stones
of the spiritual path
are smeared with muddy
paw prints. It's foggy
and dismal this late Easter
afternoon. The year hasn't
turned yet. The calendar seems stuck.
My path's a trail gone cold.
Where are the jowly bloodhounds,
loping clumsily and baying,
red-eyed as old alcoholics?
Each twist of barbed wire
and blown leaf tweaks the psyche.
Every sweet-pea blossom's
shriveled to a pastel wisp.
Yet this roll call of sights:
the trampoline, the obese
goldfish in the lily pond,
the grove-covered hills
in the distance, various
short-lived insects,
my impatience and eyestrain,
the paper plates on the picnic
table, the canary weed I'm
allergic to, that outline
of a drowned fisherman
I keep seeing: all seem
to have gained weight. How
anyone could lighten
himself enough to rise
today is a mystery.

A Measured Joy

Brilliant as fish scales,
brisk as a goat's beard:
you're a flagrant earthly
glory. Mysterious as opium
milked from the bases
of flaming immodest blossoms
whose business it is to bite
the will in two while
kissing the eyelids.
Heady as a sentence nine
miles long. Peculiarly
circuitous as the flight
path of the question-mark
butterfly. Solemn as fourteen
brown glass vials of antique
pain reliever—still potent
though no one believes it.
Patient as the self-repair
practised by myriad cloud
forms. Wild and surprising
as a scourge made of lettuce
leaves. Powerful as those
tattered books buried under
ancient temple floors,
dictated by female oracles
prophesying beautiful,
endless, elaborate disasters.
As full of epiphanies
as a thoughtful drinker.
Hilarious as a hall of feathers.

Because you roam the earth,
my having been given
a face to peer out of—
the means to witness your
trajectory—seems, if not
an outright blessing,
at least a stroke of such
luck that it reduces me
to this gibberish,
a bit like the woman
who carried her lover's
spare glass eye in her
breast pocket at all times.
Do I need to say how drastic,
elastic, and frightening love
in its lunatic ceaselessness is?

Request

A hundred years hence,
if some version
of the given world
still exists,
I'd like to meet you
all over again, dear,
in the winter home
of black-necked cranes,
amidst glassy patches
of frozen grass.
The birds would stare rudely,
eyes emitting
a glittering mineral glare,
designed to register
gnats' infinitesimal acrobatics.
We'd stand motionless
as the seasons changed, as
our hearts, slowed by cold
and later enlivened by thaw,
turned first to wrought iron,
then bent themselves
into perfect treble clefs.
Perhaps hell will have frozen
over by that late date,
posing no further threat.
Orchids and alpine flowers,
with their riot of color,
will carpet the yak pastures.
With the sincerity
of wild cranberries,

I hope, at that moment
of gradual, future warming,
that your resistence
to my well-intentioned advances
has thinned to an obstacle
I can simply bite through
with a delicate snap,
like a rice cracker.
I pray you'll no longer
refuse my adoring overtures
as we pass through bamboo forests
populated by monkeys
who shower us with bruised fruit
and human babies they've kidnapped,
who tumble into our arms, unharmed.
You'll allow me to lead you
where travelers seldom venture,
into a vine-covered temple
that suddenly becomes visible
through tattered mists.
There, leaning against
some well-curtained
inner sanctum's red doorway,
we finally begin kissing,
and you're so overcome
it takes you forever to notice
the room is on fire.

Montage of Disasters

Where's the eloquence in all this?
The train lurched, shuddered, and snapped in two.
No one knew for sure how the fire started.
Then the virus got into the milk supply.
Women went hysterical. Men wept. Children
stood dazed, caked with mud,
sucking on splintered pickets
or bits of weather vane.
Bombing destroyed much of the zoo,
freeing the animals that survived it,
which explains the lion in the subway tunnel,
grinning crocodiles new orphans watched
slither into fountains by the ruined library.
An entire cemetery washed into the river.
Nuns poured stiff jolts of whiskey
into paper cups for sooty rescue crews.
Later, it rained frogs. Bodies were laid
out on the football field, in sheeted
rows, just beyond the goalposts.
Monday morning a meteorite crashed
through a window and turned my side
of the bed to a tidy pile of cinders.
Mrs. Phipps, reading in her berth,
felt the ship rock slightly
and heard a grating sound from somewhere
under the starboard bow. I wondered
why the dog kept lunging
at that trash barrel day after day
till he tipped it over and out fell
this manicured hand. The women

caused an awful lot of trouble
in the lifeboats that night.
One lesson we learned was this:
you cannot cut corners when building a dam.
Radiation from the nearby uranium mine
caused tarantulas in the basin
to grow hundred of times their normal size.
The dead bodies began to glow, bluely.
A false sunset from the waterfront rouged
survivors' slack faces, as looters
began to work the ruins. We first met,
oh, it seems lifetimes ago, staggering
through fog banks, dodging columns of oily
smoke, wandering the city in singed pajamas.

Song

Let me assure you my hallucinations
were beautiful. Car windows liquified,
becoming small waterfalls. Prayers rose,
faint as a baby's fragrant breaths,
from a blackberry pie as the knife
pierced its crust. Plants chatted
sotto voce about "lasting things."
Drunk businessmen giggled and hit
each other with briefcases.
A bowl of lemons snored adorably.
When special sightedness allowed
me to see how people really look
beneath their silly clothes,
no one appeared dismal or wilted.
Naked, they all looked fine
in their hides, taut-skinned
as frogs, staunch as monuments.
Something charming and dark crawled
out of my mouth. Someone dear has been
restored to me. Flashing scissors
clipped the silk strings of my misgivings.
A mild little man insisted I kiss
his hardworking donkey's forehead.
I complied. I don't have to explain myself.
You understand, my readers, my dears:
man with a green thumb who's all ears,
girl locked in a closet for years,
elephant attendant, Russian hospice nurse,
picture bride married off
not for better but for worse.

In this glazed, elated hour,
the map of the promised land
tattooed on the back of my hand
in purples, greens, and reds,
is eloquent. The day will finally
arrive when we know whose grip
we are in, who owns the explosives.
But we can't make that day come.
We must wait for it.

Mixed Messages

Hi. I sketch dead fish for a living.
The ichthyologist, my boss, pickles
them, then flops one onto my desk.
I draw the fluted fins, ragged gill
slits, astonishing iridescent
mosaic of scales, the unexpected whiskers.
Though I get praise and frequent
raises, it's not a job that fills me
with much of a sense of blessedness.
Mother's handwriting got bigger
and wilder as the letter progressed,
but you know how she suffered:
life was so different after
father's regime was overthrown.
This dunce cap's a little snug.
Wouldn't your crown fit me better?
I respectfully request you take
this long-standing curse off
my soon-to-be-shaved head.
He always got stomach cramps
in the throes of physical love.
Then, emptied, with sleep overtaking
him, he'd feel the need to turn
upside down and be reborn.
The sinister fry cook looked like
Satan in a white apron, standing
rigid behind his grill, the grease
stains on his bib a lively array
of disquieting signs. He brandished
the none-too-shiny spatula, waiting

to flip my halibut steak. She wept
openly outside the bowling alley then,
expressing her flat brown sentiments,
her boring rage and regrets, so I
shoved her up against the wall
to show I understood exactly
what she meant. Later, she tried
unsuccessfully to take my temperature
or pulse, I forget which one,
by running her fingers repeatedly
over my tongue. Those fingertips
were still wet when this was written.

My Hero

What is he by nature?
A fugitive with a squint.
Someone trained to spray paint slogans
on walls in Greek and in Hebrew.

A boy admonished by his mother
to chew more slowly, to become mute.
One whose pockmarked beauty
trumpets a deafening eloquence.

An infectious melancholy.
A din, a rush of blood to the head.
This aficionado of train wrecks,
soul scribbled on like a page from a hand-me-down primer,

may be a male ray of daylight, bringing pale
forgiveness to the unwashed kitchen window.
Eyes distant and a little sad,
his shirt's sewn of pine bark—it rasps cruelly as he moves.

Maker of mincemeat. Sneerer.
Circumcision victim
whose pencil is never idle,
enthusiastic sketcher of waterfowl,

obsessed by untying knots.
Gifted with the manners
of one raised among
Bronze Age nomads,

he wears the perfume
of Hades as aftershave,
makes me feel faint
when he states:

"I read those tea leaves
quite differently."
Loathe to press the flesh, ever,
living most of his life at night

like a fire-colored toadstool,
he's smart as an egg timer,
bright-eyed as a shot glass,
ethical as shipments of counterfeit penicillin,

his opinions intricately thatched
as a collection of birds' nests.
Many times a day, he closes like a lotus at sunset . . .
now, isn't that romantic?

A Love Story

By the time I met them,
it was a sexless marriage.
They were very open about it.
A peculiar illness had taken
hold of him. Then certain
mystical elements enveloped her,
which surprised them both,
and kept her sane amidst
intermittent trickles of pain
and floods of irritation.
Her hair was quite white,
her speech, confident and musical.
They said it helped to grow
their own vegetables. Crispness
had become important.
I asked how they'd met.
He said she'd given him a ride home
from an anthropology lecture
in college. "I had to fall for
a gal who drove around listening
to tapes of pygmies singing."
She made a list of all the wild,
immoral things she was too timid,
unwilling, or old to do.
On the dresser, a bottle
of champagne was chilling
in a bedpan. Although darkness
pursued the lucky couple,
it did not catch them. When she
went into the kitchen to make

coffee, he showed me a faded
snapshot of her as a girl.
He was using it for a bookmark.
Big-eyed, bundled up, wearing a
stocking cap with a tassel,
she was licking one end
of a long, pointy icicle,
grinning.

A Fan Letter

Dear Literary Hero,

Now that you've gently
slit open my envelope,
you see naked before you
on this plain drugstore stationery
watermarked with my tears,
the shaky handwriting of one
who has been given a second chance
and desires to use it wisely.
Allow me to tell you a little
about myself. Before I was wiped
clean as the gilt-edged mirror
in my favorite gas station
lavatory—in other words,
prior to being remade
into a reflective, immaculate being
by ingesting physician-approved
chemicals, potent as the emollients
in lemon-scented furniture polish—
I felt compelled to sleep
with a grim local widower's
limp twin sons. Then I digressed
to the widower. Still unsatisfied,
I found myself eyeing
his shaggy Scottish deerhounds,
at which point I thought it best
to leave town quietly, by midnight bus,
and take up residence where
I wouldn't continue to shame

my prominent family, dashing
their political ambitions.
Brimming with remorse,
I legally changed my name
and that same night tried
to end my life in bungalow 444
of a cheap roadside motel
called The Log Cabin,
by consuming fool's parsley,
a fungus containing
several toxic compounds.
I didn't even get high.
Dread left a taste in my mouth
like old-fashioned cough syrup
flavored with horehound.
One of my cheeks
went perpetually red.
The other remained deathly pale.
I began to hang around
with old beer drinkers, to want
to lie down all the time.
I noticed a bubbling sensation
around my navel, which emitted
a squeaky hiss, as though
I were a punctured tire
leaking air. It became apparent
my poor tongue, which looked
like a dried orange peel,
was suddenly eight or nine inches
too long, an infirmity

which interfered with wound-licking
and wallpaper-tasting.
Yours truly was in a bad way!
I craved meals of charcoal
and discarded tea bags, but consoled
myself with the contents
of coffee shop ashtrays. Doors
became my nemesis—I had to
unhinge them or become unhinged
myself. Then, in the hospital,
one of the meanest ward nurses
had your recent book sticking out
of her huge, shabby purse.
I filched it, just to get
under her skin. Was I surprised,
upon opening your tome and perusing
the first paragraph, to realize
my dark days were almost over.
These pages contained my salvation.
I read and recovered. Your sentences
gave me the kick in the teeth I
sorely needed. The voice of your thoughts
woke me like a rooster announcing
the end of the world, or maybe
a raven who'd grown teeth and learned
to warble bawdy songs. Your seething words
cured me—reading each was like swallowing
leaf after leaf of a blessed, healing salad
made from ambrosia and ragweed.
I think we should meet. Every night

I stare at the photo of you
on your book's back flap, sitting
in a brocade overstuffed armchair,
smoking your pipe that resembles
a boar's tusk. I close my eyes
and perceive myself curled up
so cozily in your lap, and after that
I see the bright mayhem
of millions of fireworks,
lighting up the dark sky
of our like minds.

Four Meditations on an Ice Puddle

I.
The land you walk on today
emerged from under ancient ice—
brilliant ice under a cloudless
sky. Now the sky's crimson,
now violet, tinged with the first
delicious whiffs of nightfall.
Two thousand years ago a forest
breathed deeply here. Take heart.
Maybe the glaciers will come back.

II.
The prophetic bluish calm
that ice contains can inhabit
you too. You are full of musical
glaciers creaking and sighing.
Think on the history of salt licks,
their stubborn whiteness,
a bracelet of clear unmeltable gems,
elephant bones, bales of snowflakes.
Contemplate the strangeness
of a fish's wavering world.
How much is frozen here,
in you, in those you love,
safe and sound,
preserved for eternity?

III.
There are sudden canyons,
dripping springs, dancing gnats,
a cow licking sweet icicles
of maple sap. There are days
of nothing but silence
like a carpet woven of ice
needles. There's lengthening moss,
the amazing shape of clouds cutting
across our mountain's summit.
One must investigate the sleeping
habits of animals in winter—what
secret stores nourish
them during that protracted
sluggish time. Peer into
the glacier's magnetic glow:
mesmerizing, weirdly blue,
luminous, a frozen tide of light.
Is this a window into the depths
of the earth? Or is it a shifting
glimpse—glazed, radiant, unafraid—
of the life of the mind?

IV.
A chorus of frogs wakes you
and much later the burbling

of hundreds of tufted puffins
lulls you to sleep. Behind
your closed eyes, a pale crane
steps delicately through
thin pond ice, causing
an almost inaudible glassy
crunch: the sound of lost hours.
A handsome pair of wolves
recline on the opposite bank—
nervous, alert, resting
alongside the icefall.
A green flash, a blue flash,
the stars feel very near,
and you and your fellow travelers
turn east, toward home.

On the Road

Bear in mind all journeys
are perilous. I didn't really
know where I was when I emerged
from the woods, but something
told me to keep walking.
From far away, their remote home
resembled an ornate tiered
wedding cake, beginning to mold.
It snowed all day, flakes big
and pretty as an albino drag queen's
false eyelashes. In anticipation
of the thaw I spent the afternoon
unplugging their rain gutters.
I'd take breaks to get warm
by stepping into the barn,
which was full of snoring cows
with ice-crusted nostrils.
The hayloft felt like a giant
nest. Oh, the eggs it could
have contained! The light
was gray and faint. I thought
I smelled mint jelly,
but knew that was impossible,
though the cows' breath
did have a sweet domestic scent
to a vagrant like me. They were
in the habit of splitting kindling
in their living room that winter.
They asked me to dinner, insisting
I remove my sodden boots first,

though I worried about splinters.
Does anyone want second
helpings of rattlesnake chili
or is it time to bring out
the salamander pudding?
I woke early the next morning,
eager to leave, and found
that while I was sleeping
they'd filled my boots
with strawberries.

Blown Out

Since everyone says that you're dead,
I send you this message by a tame bird,
who was once a nervous pulsing lizard . . .
so the text's beak-dented. I'm sorry.
We're repeatedly crammed into ill-
fitting bodies we must soon struggle
out of. Is that how it works? You've
had your quick and fiery finale—
arson in the carnival of the head—
an impressive explosion and the whirling
Ferris wheel's an ash heap in fifteen
minutes. A radio astronomer drones on
about how fragile comets are.
The bed's so hot I can hardly lie down.
I pick at the sheets. Distant noises
keep me wired all night, ready to receive
any crackling, coded word from you.
Fluid shadows skitter across
the dim windows. Dizzy silence.
I'm frightened I've somehow sucked up
your symptoms. Everybody's behaving
strangely in your wake. You're not
imagining it. Physical existence,
that fucking whirlpool, oppresses
the best of us. So, what's the antidote?
Drink mustard or soapsuds?
Kiss someone with a mouth
as dirty as yours was, so I can be
a gold miner again, shoveling my tongue

through the muck to reach your gleam?
Will that ease my tarnished grief,
bring lasting peace? The worried eyes
that went defiantly silver in pictures
are gone. Can't you send word back,
via a procession of ants, a chorus
of frogs, some bubble that bursts in my
forehead, from wherever you leapt?

The Superior Man

The superior man can sit
quietly, cross-legged,
watching bees dance
above a field
of fuzzy goldenrod for hours,
without once being overcome
by the toxic melody
of his own uselessness.
This being may exit
his body on a moment's
notice, in midsentence
if necessary, without
anyone being the wiser.
Occassionally, he sucks
rusty nails when feeling
anemic. As often as not,
scholars tell us,
the superior man was a good-
looking woman—her infinite
tenderness manifest
in the way she cut her steak
or shook hands at first
meeting. A stooping, pale,
talkative figure, prone
to singing, his or her
three-colored breath remained
free of any scent of disease
and the domesticated taint
of household smoke.
The superior man picks up

a weathered shoe heel
nearly buried in the dust
of the road, and sniffs it.
His laughter is like water
that has been exposed to
starlight. He converses
easily with the ghosts
of those who were killed
by being hit over the head.
He has a taste for yellow
mushrooms that grow on dung.
He loves unerringly.
Long ago, three cities waged
a savage war to win
the privilege of burying
his ashes within their walls.
Confess! You have been cruelly
teasing me, master. You are he,
here now, in this topless bar,
one hand fiddling with
the toothpick in your drink,
the other frightened hand grazing
my thigh. It was you all along.

Psychotown

How is this village different from all others?
Simmered in the broth of unsalted gossip,
it's a well-guarded enclave where we pass
our enforced winter rest. We recover our
submerged selves here. One soul-chomping
goblin after another is hauled up from
our depths, blinking and sputtering
like litters of siblings nearly drowned
at a picnic—their bloated faces so scary
father's hair went entirely white six minutes
after a glimpse, whilst our dear mother
has lisped ever since. Later, the evacuation
of the ballet school put an end to our formal
education. Everyone walks the streets affected
by slight curses: toothache, seeing double,
dry mouth, or they're wrongly convinced
they've got syphilis. After a few days here,
some visitors sense their presence of mind
leaking from their right ear. Others find
they leave a small pink stain wherever they sit.
You've been chanting uncharacteristic wishes
in your sleep. I lived in this region all
my formative years. If you truly desire my hand
in marriage (*here he fell to his knees
in anguish as she lowered her voice to utter
her demands*), you will have to submit
to the ritual pinpricking, and let the wedding
take place in that sooty church with the artichoke-
shaped spires you can just make out jutting up
from the besmirched, yet somehow cloudless horizon.

Her Account of Herself

Born at the onset
of this tranquilizer age,
I spent decades awakening,
wandering this nation's
dazzling displays
of petticoats and neckties.
I grew into a needle-nosed
scribbler, a tight-lipped
wallflower seated between
lively philistines at banquets
and sacrifices. Such am I:
a barren head-hanger,
a secret rabbit breeder,
addicted to bonbons
and collecting botanically
accurate hand-tinted
etchings of flowering cacti
since time out of mind.
I kept my legs crossed
just as instructed,
for a hideously long time.
I still have trouble telling
the difference between
progress and pathology,
hate getting my face wet,
will not eat banana squash,
learned to ride a bike
at twenty, experience
difficulty warming up.
Were there a museum of me,

it might contain my fur muff,
my pup's first leather collar,
necklaces I made as a child
by stringing watermelon seeds,
my hearing aid, five mother-
of-pearl buttons from my unhappy
grandmother's blouse
(she never wanted to marry,
but got pregnant, and that
was that), a lopped-off ponytail,
a red eucalyptus leaf
that stuck to the windshield
of one I unsuccessfully loved,
my pocket watch, and the tub of
sweet grease I use
to groom my terrible hair.
I've often sought asylum,
remained unseduced by food,
planted a kiss on the wall
by the landing where the turn
in the stairs is called
the "coffin corner."
I'm nothing if not
cheerfully morbid, or so
my friends claim.
Call upon me if you need
contact with that breezy,
self-conscious type of turmoil
that chases its tail all day,
forming little whirlwinds.

Introducing: The Clouds

Introducing: the clouds.
Billowing, tufted,
or ragged. Flying,
or just hanging around
in the sea of air
that bathes all living
things.

Introducing: chewing gum.
With your current total
of four teeth, I'd avoid
it for the time being.
It smells nice, but makes
your jaw tired.

Introducing: insects.
Yucca moths. Fairy moths.
Paper wasps. Fat caterpillars.
Luscious stinkbugs. Some
have wings or hairy legs,
spin webs, or sting.
Others eat books or wood
or light up, manufacture
silk, or look like tiny
armored cars.

Introducing: a haircut.
A towel around your neck.
Endless mirrors. Chill
stork-beaklike scissors

flash and clip harmlessly.
Afterward, it itches
a little. The truth
is revealed: you have
beautiful pink ears
just like your uncle.

Introducing: soup.
Delicious with crumbled
crackers or croutons
flung into it. Bisque.
Consommé. Cream of green
peas. You get to use
a bigger, rounder spoon.
Gumbo. Turnip or potato
puree. A lake in a bowl,
suitable for very small
sailboats only.

Sworn Statement

We are chaff, Your Honor.
We are grass, we are mulch,
we are unseasoned bread crumbs.
There is plenty of evidence:
blood on her pants cuff,
a rusted wheelbarrow brimful
of blood, skin fragments
under her fingernails,
the nail beds blue as gas.
The door to her bridal chamber
hung from its hinges. Hah!
We entered and saw:
the aforementioned defendant
lying in a grove of beautiful
appetizing trees and good-
smelling shrubs, smoldering,
licked at by the wise fire
of intelligence, panged
by hunger. She had fallen within
a ring of salt, under a prearranged
plan, covered lightly by some silky
whims, while a searchlight played
over the scene. We men are stalwart;
women, jealous. It's the way
of the world. Night after night
she slipped out of her bedroom
into our suite and made us
do what we didn't want to do.
Afterward, we never recognized
ourselves, not even while shaving

the next morning. One should
not suppress yawning. One
should be kind to insects.
One should not ride an untamed
animal. One should assist invalids,
remain chaste, avoid strong rushing
water. Women itch like the site
of an old injury. They ache
in spring, in cold weather,
have trouble keeping still,
pressing their silly knees
together. The bishop's wife,
here on trial in absentia,
dreamed of a pig cavorting
in the dining room. She chuckled
sweetly in her sleep.
That laughter, like the voice
of one who cries out from afar,
led us astray.

Dog World

It's hard to be human.
Doomed to tumble
into troubled sleep
every morning near dawn;
when slumber finally engulfs you
it's like being pushed down a well.
After a long fall you hit
lead-colored water, thrash around,
churning up muck, and nearly drown
in doubts about your sanity,
bank account, and having
kissed someone you shouldn't
on a lunch break you weren't
supposed to take, anyway.
Face it. You've always
been more comfortable
in the company
of fun-loving Welsh corgis,
brainy German shepherds,
contemplative basenjis,
or solemn Neopolitan mastiffs,
whose ageless wrinkled faces,
labyrinths of noble folds,
resemble ancient Sumerian kings'
fabled ultrasaggy genitalia.
Welcome to a land where urine
is sacrament; where knowledge
equivalent to that contained
in man's vast, dusty libraries
can be gleaned immediately,

through your nose. Rabbits
abound in this other world
you've woken up into, popping
out of the underbrush
like bubbles from champagne.
No more fretting about
your hairline. You have beautiful
mahagony markings now
and a spotted belly,
the same as your litter sister,
who (unlike the aloof women
in that cowboy bar last night)
will be happy to have quick,
energetic sex with you,
whenever you wish. Crisp, wiry hair
covers your form. Your tail
is long and strong. This kingdom
of wet paws, of romps through miles
of bluebells and red alder,
of dizzying sunlight and powdery
snowdrifts to roll in, is animated by
the irresistible glint
in a pheasant's cold golden eye,
the pleasure of tearing
anything to bits with your teeth,
of scaring raccoons away from
a half-eaten hamburger and french fries;
or of falling instantly, peacefully
asleep in a hayloft, your mouth full
of crunchy, succulent twigs.

Jews

What does a Jew want?
Excellent question.
It depends on the hour.
In the morning he needs
an unobstructed view
of that ant farm,
the underworld,
and a magnifying glass,
so he can observe
suffering in miniature.
In the afternoon
he requires a stack
of curious documents
to read and a sack
of poppy seeds. Every evening:
the comforts only a woman
can give. On a daily basis
he craves feeling the great pain
in his chest melt away while crying
intensely salty tears that pepper
his beard. Lots of clean, rough towels.
Not to be tempted into limping
after that Christ guy, seeking
a pat on the head, restitution,
some stupid excuse or a belated
invitation to supper. He aspires
to lead a guilt-free and holy life—
never to awaken besmeared
with the greenish-brown ointment
of evil. He prays to retain

the fire flickering in his eye
and to recognize it in the gaze
of others. To sit down
to a breakfast so hearty it makes
his innards ache, and after that
to hand out fried-egg sandwiches
to hungry passersby. To grant
a sexual exception every time
he meets another sad-eyed woman
dressed in the colors of field
or sky and to sleep with her
immediately. To remove his pious
black clothes, wildly excited
by the mournful universe
in female form swaying
naked before him. While he's
on top of her, he visits
the little motherland in his head,
full of industrious wasps,
tumblers of cognac, his love
of electric lights
and intellectual resistance.
His wife's virtues,
shrill in his ears
like violin strings.
He groans with delight,
losing himself in the tangle
of the strange woman's hair,
and in the glint of conscience
gleaming beneath her overcast

glance. He thinks of the lives
of the stars—they're born
whitely and die in red.
Is that a trickle of blood
on her thigh? Alas, one
cannot have everything.

Group Portrait, with Pitchforks

The sullen glare in our eyes,
a form of national sadness,
must not be taken lightly.
Our brows, furrowed as any ploughed
farm plot, are raked and ready
to be reseeded. Isn't a dismal,
wizened visage part of our dark charm?
Little whittled carvings of a native
mountain god adorn our hearths.
His name sounds like a yell for help
from the depths of a bad dream.
Face blue with lust, he sports
the itchy, sore buds of just-erupting
horns on his forehead; also hooves
and a corkscrew tail. Our scrawny women
are victims of continual sniffles,
especially on raw mornings before the sun,
boiling up like runny egg yolk,
drips orange over the horizon.
All our thoughts are born in our stomachs,
so we keep our teeth clamped together.
Otherwise, wild ideas hanging upside down
inside us, fermenting all night,
might escape and fly, batlike and black,
out of our mouths. The taste
of this daily self-restraint
is that of soured, boot-bruised
flower petals: *pink verbena,*
prickly thrift, meadow orchid,
traveler's joy. These cheerily

named plants were christened long ago,
before the ocean was known to us,
when the graveyard seemed vacant—
its few rough stones iced
with a light picturesque snow;
when you could still lean
your back against a chaste tree
in a freezing rain and hope
to be washed clean.

Chain of Events

I wanted a corpse,
and though the previous
week there had been piles
of them stacked
in the high school gym,
I was given only kindling
and fuzzy plaid blankets.
Perched on a bar stool
not long after a major
earthquake, I cried out
for a stiff drink
and felt instead
an awful substitute,
strong emotion,
filling me as though
poured from on high
into a hole drilled
through the top of my head,
only to leak out the soles
of my feet. Not again!
I'd promised to swallow
anything forbidden or prescribed
in order to quit worrying
so intensely about *virtue:*
its crisp mystery, endless rules,
eleventh-hour self-punishment
sessions. I just wanted
to get drunk and clear my head
of the slop of recent events.
Spend a year musing

(fueled by Kahlua and a twilight
cast of mind) about obscure
subjects: aphrodisiacs
for example; or whether
hot or cold water
best removes wine stains
from cotton sheets;
how tasty hardened drops
of glue seemed in elementary
school; the history of jewelry.
Finally my drink arrived.
The liquid looked nearly black
in the weird light, the color
of the infernal, ignorance,
and long mourning.
Time to ingnite the gut fire,
my pilot light. The first sip
put a bright border around
whatever I stared at. The second
touched off an urge to pour
the rest down the white collar
of the man sitting next to me
whose hair looked like
deerskin or mouse fur,
but his cough, a sound akin
to that of a baby's rattle,
stayed my hand. The more I drank
the more drained I felt.
I had to drink faster.
A grimy, shell-shocked

youngster wearing her torn
blouse inside out
clambered into my lap,
putting a damper
on my ability
to behave as uncouthly
as I usually look forward
to doing in bars.
I patted her back between
shoulder blades no bigger
than toast points,
my approximation
of a motherly touch.
She grabbed my patting
hand, stuck the fingers
in her mouth
and began sucking them,
as though something might
be dredged up from this dead
well, as though weak milk
thin as cactus juice
might flow from under my nails
if she sucked hard enough—
as though instead of
an empty mine shaft barely
moistened by liquor,
I was some sort of spigot.

Crown of Weeds

(after John Ruskin)

Having nothing to love in my solitary
boyhood, I had seen no grief. My friends
were the intricate carpet design
on the stairs, lizards, a particular
configuration of branches. All my delights
were based in these acute, complicated tastes.
I bloomed manic, strange. If I'd been born
invisible, or bodiless, as long
as I retained the analytic faculty
of sight, my appreciation of color
and pattern, I'd have suffered much less.
But God chose to shove me
onto the battlefield of my family,
society, and the fairer sex, unarmed.
Consequently, at this late date,
having buried both parents, aging rapidly,
I remain more or less defenseless.
Voice rough and tuneless,
my eyebrows grow shaggy and my hair's
shot through with dignified
silver I'll never merit.
Much of me is dead, but more of me
is stronger. I still consume the world
with my eyes: cathedrals, weeds,
cabbage leaves, nine-year-old girls.
Nearly a year ago, at the spot
marked by the twisted stump
on this windblown cliff,

a huge blackness swept over me—
battering passions I thought
I'd recovered from, which,
when acknowledged, made me feel
skinned and sick. I tried to leap
the railing and escape,
momentarily forgetting the pleasure
ahead of me, on the hike back
to my ugly house, of crunching pebbles
under my boots. I'll live
a little longer, after all.
It's still early. When I return,
they'll be making pancakes.

The Wanderer

The wanderer's tongue thrusts out
of his mouth like something alive
independent of him—an eyeless
groping creature who knows bile,
the rubbery flavor of egg yolk,
and bitter tidbits of harbor barnacle.
Cloaked in his loneliness, he smells
of dogs mating and duckweed.
He seeks a hospitable fireside
before nightfall; failing that,
a haystack. The sky's white now;
it's trying to snow. Will he sleep
in a drift? It won't be the first time.
He recognizes important trees
when he sees them. His shoes
belonged to a man recently deceased,
a parting gift from the widow.
His eyes are the green of the sea
before its waters get threatening.
A fruitful disorder characterizes
his mind. Remote groves and streams
feed and water his thoughts,
so his pulse is a torrent.
Tattered, thirsty, he's taking long
strides. The clerical crows
are his black-clad companions.
Under their influence, he believes
it's essential, every day, at all
costs, to make one's love known.

Nowadays

The dead simply won't stay dead
anymore. They trudge ten paces
behind the living,
dragging extinct feet,
lowing like cows,
stinking like fried liver.
I've lost the ability
to be comforted.
Many's the time she lay
her cool hand
on my sweaty brow
and suggested: "Meditate
on those parts of you
which must eventually die
and the one part that never will."
But each time I took
a groping inventory,
nothing in me reared up
on its hind legs
to declare itself immortal.
To the tune of my shopworn
internal organs' dumb
factory hum, I stared
at the peach fuzz
on her upper lip,
and fought the urge
to kiss her.
At times like these,
one wants more music,
less carping and grousing,

a sip of team spirit to light up
the dank gullet, then blossom
fiery and bright in the stomach
like gin does. We seek reverie,
that vision-dimmer, a tinkling
melody recalling the crumbled
white cliffs of the past,
the familiar lump that lodged
in your throat, when, showing off
at Thanksgiving dinner,
you tried to swallow several
cannonball olives whole.
Men go out of their way nowadays
to smell like spareribs,
and we women never say anything
that makes a shred of sense.
That's why we're buried
with a chunk of sod
or a thick songbook
wedged under our chins,
to remind us that in the grave
we're under a weighty obligation
to keep quiet and refrain
from disturbing our neighbors—
both those interred next to us,
and the souls still stomping
around above ground, biting
their grubby fingernails,
which refuse, despite sacrifices
and bribes, to cease growing.

Cul-de-sac

Here the things of the past
come to an end.
Useless longings
that gave off such a whiff
of brimstone, from which
arms of flame once shot
hundreds of feet into the air,
alarming the populace
and laying waste to acres
of charming native vegetation . . .
well, let's just say these yearnings
have shriveled considerably.
While still kindled
in me, they're now composed
solely of secondhand light
not unlike the moon's:
silvery gray,
damning as faint praise,
insipid as dishwater.
I have even less to offer
than I did years ago,
when you disappeared.
My paltry effects include
a series of sacred earaches,
a Styrofoam life preserver
lifted from an ocean liner,
a photo of King Kong
in a dress suit, and tales
from a wedding night
spent rolling around

in a famous Confederate
battlefield's scratchy
blood-fed weeds.
Erosion rakes the face
of a distant stone cliff
where an ancient master race
carved a vertical city.
They worshiped bearded
river gods hidden under
cattails and algae in deep
ravines miles below. Nature's
radiance flares and pales.
I have no intention of being
direct. Fearing the worst,
I send you this missive—
an ill-tempered penance,
on stationery edged with motifs
of huge saw-toothed glaciers
and crunchy little runner beans.
The letterhead pictures
all I've tickled or sipped
since we parted. O landlord
of my heart, must love always
end with a thud? Won't you
appear in one of the gaping
holes in this prose—
stick your head out of a crater
in this minefield of writing,

so I can grab a handful
of your hair and sink my teeth
into your ear like
some fleshy hors d'oeuvre?

Commentary

*"Every blessed
or blasted object's got
a mind of its own now,
a peevish will of iron.
The tin spoon's blank face
glints openly, meanly.
Clothing and skin develop
an adversarial relationship.
Each new item's designed
not to satiate but to create
worse need, baser fears.
The beverage dribbling
down your chin like quicksilver
intensifies thirst. Newfangled
bandages increase bleeding——"*

The ancient clay tablet
breaks off here, but we know
how this grievance ends
from corroborating texts.
Sleep blows over
the long-winded
complainer like a wet haze,
causing him to forget
the body and its little
problems, his minor
quibbles with the spirit
of his age. The clamor
in the field of rushes
across the stream

grows louder and wakes him.
He attends a party
at the summer palace,
but will not permit any
of the guests to approach
him. Later that night,
sequestered in his drafty
attic, he writes his famous
suite of "Four Serious Songs,"
the first of which begins:
"How dare you have fun
in my absence!" and jots
down notes for what was
later to become his lively,
timeless cycle entitled
"Sixty Miseries," with
its many witty references
to boundary stones,
the fishing net, a grab
bag lined with thorns,
and the mysterious victim
dug up by dogs, which
we will consider
in some detail
in the following chapter.

The Underworld

The exhausted dead lean on silvery pillars.
The frilly scent of pear blossoms mixes
easily with the heavier smells of fried food
that hang jagged, spiking the air
like invisible stalactites. There *is*
a river. Women who murdered their husbands
with hairpins study Plato daily.
Saints are encouraged to complain at length,
to dress better, sweeten their anxious,
famished breath by gumming mint leaves.
Horizons broaden. The pear blossoms wither
and drop off. Hard little knobs of fruit swell
underneath. Harmless, noiseless swordplay
takes place. There are plenty of figs
to use in making nice sticky brown jam.
Pigs squeal throughout. Bedrooms are decorated
in either the fierce heraldic hues
of an ancient age or all nineteen
shades of white identified by the Eskimos,
a color scheme even the recalcitrant dead,
who refuse to rise, find surprisingly reviving.

Dry-eyed Survivor

The priest fainted when he saw
the looks on our liberators' faces.
While we civilians cowered and prayed
in our basements, they hid a wounded
lieutenant in a haystack to keep him
from freezing. It was the lieutenant's
idea. One of his last brainstorms. He
was furious he couldn't smoke inside
the dry pile of fodder. "My rustic
refuge," he sang in our language,
with a terrible accent and chocolate
on his breath. His tongue was violet.
Whole regiments had been summarily
buried in our village, using gun butts
for shovels. As the thaw commenced,
we children would trip over frozen
soldiers' heads emerging from melting
snow like a macabre crop of pumpkins.
Bathing became an unbelievable luxury.
Those of us who were eleven or twelve
fell into sex early: one hand clapped
over your mouth and another shoved
down your pants. I remember
being yanked down in a bombed-out barn,
surrounded by starving cows, by a girl
who had the skills of an acrobat
and very chapped hands. Later I lost
track of her. She had a throaty
voice and perfect proportions.

I hope this doesn't make you jealous.
I haven't thought about her in a long
time. Not since last night, right before
falling asleep. Panting and gasping,
then yelling the usual frantic
warnings in my native dialect
(which you have grown so accustomed to
but still can't translate), I woke up,
drenched in sweat. I opened my eyes.
You were lying beside me,
as always, wide-eyed, attentive,
standing guard over me while flat
on your back. You seem to do this
all night, every night, as though
you never need to sleep.

She Senses the Presence of a Dead Suitor
in Her Room

Like that unsung juncture in the dead of night
when a sleeper's mouth finally falls open,
this yawning moment stretches to form
a sort of threshold you glide through, ·
temporarily exiting the light-blasted paradise
where you now reside: the womb of everything,
where naked psyches ascend higher and higher,
till they bruise the solar system's limits;
where thoughts consort with other thoughts
that have always adored them; and faithful
sweethearts grapple, for eternity, on beds
of fallen oak leaves. When I foam at the mouth
a little, I know you're really in the vicinity,
about to pay a visit to the world from which you
recently retreated, realm of pork chops
and chromosomes, plowed fields and glider pilots,
torrential rain and that ache in one's trousers.

This world came about through a terrible mistake.
I fell into your arms in much the same way.
When you were alive, the darkness rose for you.
My old dog, who trusts no one, quietly ate
a piece of bacon from your hand, then a slice
of pear. Come, dreadful one, unbegrudgingly.
Make yourself known. Groan my name. Rattle window-
panes like the blizzard did. Last night you starred
in my dream, clutching an ear-piercing device
in one hand and a heavily embroidered codpiece

in the other, your pockets bulging with rocks
in case you had to brain someone in self-defense.
Has your old home grown so frightening?
Now the reek of disquieting ideas, which often
preceded you, an olfactory ambassador,
pervades the room like a symphony
of ripening cheeses. Let's face facts:
You're my tormentor. I'm your pale weakling,
a white toothpaste smear left behind
in the bathroom sink; one last slice
of apricot pie losing its juice,
languishing uneaten on the overladen table
at your wake. So many important men eulogized
you, while scores of pleasantly scented women
wept incessantly, wiping their runny noses
on their dress hems. This love I'd hoped
would cure my bad character brought a fog on me.
What was it like those last moments,
saying good-bye to yourself? It had nothing
to do with what we think of as religion,
did it?

If you trudge back to heaven empty-handed,
alone, you'll be rewarded.
Infinite sweetness
will well up all around you.
As you retrace your steps, it will
run down the rough trunks
of winter-bitten trees—liquid
gratitude; oozy, drippy forgiveness.

It's my duty to shoo you away,
back to the pure light no one
can look into, but I won't do it.
Though my ears are full of the babbling,
sensible world, I will rise
for you, helpless as sap, if you beckon.
I'll stumble in what I intuit
is your general direction.
Please don't leave. Participate
in my face by means of kisses
it will take me years to feel.

Blur

The bright world gleams, sulky, autumnal,
its runny colors varnished with tears.
I'm listening to the radio in the kitchen,
crying, because the pope just declared
women still can't be priests.
I blow my nose loudly on a flowered
dish towel. My behavior's absurd, as usual,
a mystery even to me. Why should I care
what any church decrees? I'm not Catholic,
or religious, though I was a cloisterish
child who coveted the gothic costumes
of monks and nuns, who liked to get high
by fasting. Hunger gave my thoughts
new velocity, made each speedy idea
pulse like a cartoon drawn by a nervous
hand, ready to burst its twitchy outline,
KABOOM! and spatter my gray brains all over
mother's whitewashed walls. The notion
that a gulp of wine could turn into the blood
of a loved one was beyond erotic. I guess
I felt *temperamentally* Catholic:
morbidly fearful, my psyche wallpapered
with bleak, repeating motifs of sin
and punishment. Doesn't the pope know
the blur around the body, that constant
living light, is women's truest garment,
was St. Joan's most invincible layer
of armor? Women's skirted, ample laps
are valleys of salvation, from the moment
the crowns of our drenched infant heads

enlarge the split between their splayed
legs as we first slide into our lives
till the instant when, if we're lucky
enough, we die in some woman's sacred
embrace, patient and eternal as the moon-
yanked tide. Poor pope, blind to women's
spiritual gifts. All we females can do
is gaze into the star-flecked sky,
and reading what's written there,
dry our eyes.

To My Brother

My mind is full of you. In the tranquility
of this blizzard, I meditate on: 1. your bravery,
which takes the form of a spiky titanium halo
made of bike spokes fanned out behind your head
like a peacock's tail, which only some of us can see,
2. the aura that appears to you before seizures,
and 3. your calmness and grace in a grave
situation. You occupy my thoughts entirely,
the way snow in this place where I find myself
vacationing silently conquers the landscape
it blankets, while tall trees, rough-barked
monarchs, shiver their timbers. It's as if
the storm's voice, hollow rumblings
and swallowed washy howls, was deputized
one of your many emissaries. Everything
natural and unnatural has been drafted
as your ambassador. The wind's subliminal
engine roar is now reminiscent of your
laconic conversation—talk that's suddenly
become vital to me on a daily basis,
since I've been threatened with losing you
to a *brain tumor*—a term that last month
wouldn't have been allowed out of my mouth.
I've always been afraid to pronounce or read
names of serious diseases: bad luck
to pass my eyes over such words. Now,
thirty days post diagnosis, I've said
"brain tumor" so often it could be my cat's name.
I've started carrying a photo of you in my pocket
at all times. I show it to people. The consistent

reaction: "Oh, he's so handsome." I've got snapshots
of you hiking, skiing, or dropped to one knee
in a weedy field, flanked by your adolescent dogs.
All I'm able to perceive lately has undergone
alchemical transformation. Vague memories of you
stumbling around in diapers; my still-packed
suitcase; medical reports; or heavy-bellied clouds
rush at me, tumbling over each other
in their eagerness to testify to your continued
existence. They zoom forward, hang before me
and waver, a complicated mirage, strange
as a Hieronymus Bosch painting of limbo's
undulating landscape—equal parts darkness,
outrage, and galvanized fighting spirit.
In my new, upended life, days pass,
and the events they contain glow with the luster
of just-dug-up gold. For no good reason
it made me feel better last night when you said,
over a crackling telephone connection,
it was snowing like crazy where you are, too.

Miasma

You claim there's a road
through this nightmare terrain,
over crevice and fissure,
hill and dale of that planet
afloat in the cup of your skull—
your thoughts' native soil,
a gray world thickly crisscrossed
by little rivers, shrouded in cloud.
You survived the peeling back
of your brain's protective
membranes, one dubbed *dura mater*,
"hard mother," by early surgeons
because it's tough to cut through;
another called *arachnoid*
for its white likeness to spiderweb.
You joked drunkenly while waking
from an operation where virtuoso
neurosurgeons sliced your brain
thin as rich birthday cake. It's
gross understatement to say your path's
strewn with obstacles: the migration
of proper names, the debris of seizures,
Demerol's flapping circus tent
dizzily printed with wild red spirals,
your family's abject panic—
all this enclosed by a survival
curve's high electrified fence.
Smiling, you comfort your loved ones,
fear lodged in their throats like fish bones.
I cannot say how much I admire you,

who purified himself at a moment's notice,
though I contend you were squeaky clean
at the start. Every day you pass through
this mapless landscape unharmed,
a fruit falling to earth, so sure
of its ripeness. Your conviction's
made a believer even of me, your grim,
bewildered sister, who ought to turn
in the pile of books she's cowered
behind all her life and get in line
to become your disciple. Yes, I agree,
this miasma will evaporate,
just as you say. It will lift
like mist from the fine
blameless mind in which it began,
erased by a radiance whose source
is not glowing isotopes,
but your right and left
hemispheres, those fertile
interlocking continents,
homelands of your soul.

Colorlessness

Eventually, we all lose the perfumed,
bejeweled world, beyond which lies
silent anarchy. The yellow of burnt grass
evaporates like fumes. Poof! The green
of leeks is gone. You're robbed of the rich
ripe browns of feces, the ringing inner
pink of grilled beef. The watery gray
of writing and drawing ink fades away
too. Clear-seer, observer of matter's
never-ending attempt to reduce or augment
itself into just light, does color's flight
prefigure your coming nothingness: mud to flesh
to thin air, or will some tendril at last
burst from you: saffron, black, or earwax
orange, to scare the pants off both atheists
and verse mongers—a spindly rebellion
germinated for ages, not in follicle or marrow,
but in that maypole of our emotions: *fear*,
whose multicolored ribbons flutter
and flutter like nerves branching
from a backbone—they twitch and sting
but can never be grasped. Throughout
the pervasive gray of disgrace, the purple
of complaint, despite your alternating caresses
and attempts to shrug me off, I swear
by the reek of the dung heap, by the slip
and slide of white silk, by the feelings
you stupidly unleashed in me, I will never
lose you completely in the gathering tide
of colorlessness, due to love's stubborn tint.

Amy Gerstler is a writer of fiction, poetry and journalism, who lives in Los Angeles. Her eighth book, *Bitter Angel*, was published by North Point Press (1990), and was awarded a National Book Critics Circle Award in poetry in 1991. Her previous seven books include *The True Bride* (Lapis Press, 1986), *Primitive Man* (Hanuman Books, 1987), and *Nerve Storm* (Penguin, 1993). In 1987 she was awarded second place in *Mademoiselle* magazine's fiction contest. Her work has appeared in numerous magazines and anthologies, including *The Paris Review* and *The Best American Poetry* 1988, 1990, and 1992. Text works of hers have been performed at the Museum of Contemporary Art in Los Angeles, and elsewhere. In the fall of 1989, she collaborated on an installation at the Santa Monica Museum of Art, and a related artists' book, with visual artist Alexis Smith, both of which are titled "Past Lives." The installation traveled to the Josh Baer Gallery in New York City in December 1990. She has collaborated with her sister, choreographer Tina Gerstler, and visual artists Megan Williams and Gail Swanlund. She contributes monthly reviews to *Artforum* magazine. Her writing has appeared in catalogs for exhibitions at the Long Beach Museum of Art, Los Angeles Contemporary Exhibitions, The Whitney Museum of American Art, The Los Angeles Museum of Contemporary Art, The Fort Wayne Museum of Art (Fort Wayne, Indiana), and Security Pacific Inc. She has taught English and creative writing at Otis Art Institute, Art Center College of Design, UCLA extension, and the University of California at Irvine.